Time Does Not Heal All Wounds

How to Fight a Parole

By Kathleen Connelly Takats

First Edition

Biographical Publishing Company
Prospect, Connecticut

Time Does Not Heal All Wounds

How to Fight a Parole

First Edition

Published by:
Biographical Publishing Company
35 Clark Hill Road
Prospect, CT 06712-1011
Phone: 203-758-3661 Fax: 253-793-2618
e-mail: biopub@aol.com

First Printing 2009

PRINTED IN THE UNITED STATES OF AMERICA

Publisher's Cataloging-in-Publication Data

Takats, Kathleen Connelly
Time Does Not Heal All Wounds : How to Fight a Parole –1st ed.
p. cm.
ISBN 1929882475 (Paperback : alk. paper)
13 Digit ISBN 9781929882472
1. Homicide. 2. Victim survivor rights. 3. Fighting parole. I. Title.
Dewey Decimal System 364.152
Library of Congress Control Number: 2009925155

Contents

Dedication

In loving memory of my brother, James Frances Connelly, who touched our lives and will never be forgotten (born April, 15, 1963, murdered January 22, 1979 at 15 years old). For my parents, Barbara and James Connelly - there are no words, just prayers. To my sisters, Patti and Barbie and my brother Terry, I could not have gotten through this without you. Thank you all for your love and support.

Mission

I strongly desire to seek justice where justice is due. I will educate and prepare you for your own parole hearings with all of the data I have accumulated over the past seven years from my own experience. The loss of my brother, Jimmy Connelly, who was murdered by the hands of John Duffy, was a treacherous experience for me, my family, and our friends. This book is a guideline to help you maintain and organize a well-managed parole portfolio, which can be used for each and every hearing in your case. Please use it as a workbook to help you prepare the proper documentation to be sent to the parole commissioners. I wish you the best of luck in your fight against parole and hope your strategies prove you victorious.

"It is impossible to win the race unless you venture to run, impossible to win the victory unless you dare to battle." –Richard M. DeVos

Chapter 1
The life and death of James Connelly

My brother, James F. Connelly, was my best friend. My family and I shared an extremely close relationship with him and he had such a positive influence on our lives. We lived in the Bronx until I was ten when we moved to Long Island in 1972. Our large Irish family, consisting of five children, loved playing on the streets and running through all the buildings. As kids, we dug to China in the yard and buried money to see if it would grow. I tell my daughter that we were like "Hey Arnold" city kids. We played Monopoly for hours, gin rummy, war, and poker. Jimmy, as we always called him, was a great checker and chess player. In the summer, we all swam for hours and Jimmy proved to be the best one of all and was the most physically fit.

Jimmy and I had endless adventures. We had snowball fights on the street and Christmas caroled for our neighbors. We would sneak out of the house to join our friends at bonfires. One time, we snuck out after a huge snow storm, and Jimmy decided to bribe our dog, Polo, with food so that he would not bark and rat us out. Sure enough, Polo began to bark wildly at the sight of us and we ducked behind the nearest car to hide. Mom immediately exclaimed, "Jimmy, come inside" and I thought that I was home free. Seconds later, mom shrieked, "Kathy, you too!" We were like a comedy routine - he was Dean Martin and I was Jerry Lewis. Our fun and laughter never stopped.

I loved Jimmy with all of my heart. He really did bring peace, love, and happiness to the world with his good nature and sense of humor. He was one of my closest friends and companions and I will never forget the day that he was taken away from me. To think that our laughter, our friendship, and our lives would be destroyed instantaneously by a nineteen year old murderer is impossible for me to comprehend.

My brother was only fifteen when John Duffy, also known as John Marino, brutally stabbed him to death and consequently took a piece of my soul. My brother's body was found a day later, on January 23, 1979 by a sanitation worker. His skull was crushed and his throat had been slashed multiple times. My family was in shambles and I knew that our lives would never be the same. Fighting Duffy's parole and keeping him behind bars for life provides me with some redemption, but will never bring Jimmy back to life.

Chapter 2

My first parole experience

Twenty years later, John Duffy was up for parole. I knew I had to do something to prevent his release, but I didn't know where to begin. I knew the murder of my brother could not have been the first criminal offense that Duffy committed. I did extensive research through the Freedom of Information Act and with a private detective I found two arrests for violent behavior. One was when he assaulted a woman while on bail and the other arrest for destructing government property and resisting arrest. Both offenses occurred in Manhattan and the Nassau County District Attorney's office was unaware of these acts due to the inability to jointly track cases when different aliases were used. Consequently, Duffy's bail was not revoked in 1982. I further investigated Duffy's history from prison and discovered reports of unusual behavior. Hundreds of pages noted drug use, disorderly conduct, and contraband ranging from violent acts to directly disobeying orders. I was provided with copies of his inmate file and shared it with the New York State Parole Board. I then wrote my first parole hearing letter describing the heinous acts of Duffy and the effects it had on my family. I took further action by contacting my local newspaper for a press release which had them feature an article commemorating Jimmy's life and my mother's perseverance through such loss. My mother's picture appeared on the cover of Newsday, the day of the first parole hearing, September 11th, 2001. It was the first time Duffy was to be seen by the parole board and the article discussed our family's healing methods. For example, we took all of Jimmy's clothes and made a blanket for my mom. Many of the 9/11 victims' family members used this idea to remember their loved ones.

After all of the time and effort my family invested into keeping Duffy behind bars, he was denied parole. This was the first of many parole hearings to come and we will continue to strengthen our case in order to succeed in all future hearings. The following chapter will provide you with strategies to help you build your case in fighting parole.

Chapter 3

Strategies for a successful hearing

It is paramount that you submit and learn your rights under the Crime Victim's Board. It will help you greatly and empower you, regardless of your circumstance. Every state has a Crime Victim's Board and you are eligible to receive compensation by contacting them. Forms can be obtained from all District Attorneys' offices, hospitals, and police stations. You can also find them at this website: *http://www.cvbstate.ny.org* or by calling 1-800-247-8035 or 1-888-289-9747. If you contact your District Attorney, ask to speak with a crime victim advocate for assistance. It is his/her job to help you, and remember to be persistent to compel them to answer all of your concerns.

You can obtain criminal records and information on inmates under the Department of Correctional Services, DOCS. Every state has a Division of Parole in the DOCS that can provide you with inmate information and victim services. In New York State, the number for DOCS is 1-888-846-3469. I encourage you to request the hearing minutes of your case in order to strengthen your letters to the board.[1] In my letters, I have used John Duffy's own words against him by gathering ample evidence from the hearing minutes. In addition, contact the inmate's prison to receive copies of their behavioral reports to examine the nature of their conduct. My brother's murderer had over two hundred pages of discipline reports that I shared with parole commissioners, the community, and during a victim impact meeting. You can also request a recent photo of the inmate for your records. The policies and laws differ from state to state, so contact your local authority with any further questions you may have.

In addition to the above research strategies, press releases are available through various media sources such as television, newspaper articles, and the internet. A press release is helpful in sharing your family's story of the trauma that you have experienced and can quickly spread awareness to others regarding the parole battle you are fighting. There are internet sites and book publications on the format of press releases in order to create one with ease and effortlessness. Please be advised that you are publicly sharing your story with the media therefore you must be prepared to openly share your pain with others; if not, a different strategy should be utilized. You can contact your local newspaper or television station to publicize your parole hearing. You may also post a free blog site on the internet to discuss your upcoming hearing and to make others aware of the difficulties of parole. Numerous websites, such as "Victims can Fight Parole," "Parole Block Program," and "Parents of Murdered Children" advocate for the victim's family by circulating petitions, newsletters, and requesting letters of support for prevention of parole. The internet has thousands of support groups of those who have suffered as you have. It is important to know that you are not alone in this battle to fight parole and that the more attention that is drawn to your hearing, the better.

In preparation for the parole hearing, submit your first letter to the Victim Impact Unit and include letters from elected officials and religious affiliates to support your case. There is now a new toll-free telephone number to access the Victim Impact Unit which is

---

[1] To receive hearing minutes of inmate parole interview, go to Division of Parole Council office.

easier for the general public to use (1-800-639-2650; see the Victim Impact Policy at the end of this chapter for additional information.) Friends and relatives may also write letters to the board petitioning against the criminal's release. If you have seen a health professional for medical/psychological services for help in coping with your loss, include pertinent letters and records to solidify your case. At the top of all letters submitted, be sure to include the inmate's ID number to keep all documents in order. Below is a note that we wrote to request letters of support which also gives John Duffy's prison ID number. Feel free to use it as a template for your own note to family and friends.

June 28, 2001

Dear Family & Friends,

Please excuse me for not addressing each of you personally. Due to some recent medical conditions, I do not have access to my own computer and printer.

This is the first time we will be opposing the parole of John Duffy, the murderer of my 15-year-old son, Jimmy. My family and I would appreciate your help. Would you write a letter on our behalf?

To my friends, I hope you will not think of me as imposing on our friendship, but rather that I value it so much I feel I can appeal to you as I appeal to our extended family.

I thank all of you for this consideration.

The information is as follows:

John Duffy
NYSID
DIN#

Please send the letters to the following address:

NYS Board of Parole
Victim Impact Unit
97 Central Ave.
Albany, NY 12206

With sincere appreciation,

Barbara Connelly & Family

The same letters can be used for all subsequent hearings because the board does not always consist of the same members. As you view my letters, be sure to note the details on how they are structured. You can also create a picture board, slide show, or home video of the victim. It is beneficial for the board to see the face of your loved one to establish a visual connection between the victim's name and face. From my personal experience this has worked with good effect.

Please note after each parole hearing I request the hearing minutes from Division of Parole Council via fax. I use John Duffy's own words to prove he still lies.

All of the above strategies have provided me with great success in blocking John Duffy from parole. I hope these tools will enable you to fight your parole battle and succeed.

Victim Impact Policy

N.Y.S. Board of Parole

Victim Impact Unit – V.I.P.

97 Central Avenue

Albany, New York 12206

Introduction

It is the policy of the Board of Parole that crime victims are an integral part of the criminal justice process and that they should be treated with fairness, sensitivity and dignity at all times. The Parole Board always has taken into account any written statement received from a victim or victim's representative. In 1985, that practice was made part of New York State law, providing that victims or their representatives may submit a written victim impact statement to the Board of Parole which must then consider it, along with certain other factors, in reaching a decision to either grant or deny release on parole to an inmate. Since 1991, the Parole Board has provided for personal victim impact statements in selected cases.

Parole Overview

The Board of Parole has the power and duty of determining which inmates serving indeterminate sentences of imprisonment in the custody of the New York State Department of Correctional Services may be released on parole, when and under what conditions. The Chairperson of the 19 member Board of Parole also is the chief executive officer of the Division of Parole. The Division of Parole is the New York State agency responsible for the community supervision of offenders released from prison by actions of the Board of Parole or, statutorily, by receipt of time off for good behavior.

Inmates become eligible for discretionary release consideration by the Board of Parole when they have served their minimum sentences. If release is granted, the Board may impose special conditions upon a parolee, including conditions that they have no contact with the victim(s) of their crime and abide by the terms of any current order of protection issued by a court. Failure to comply with any condition of release may subject the parolee to revocation of release proceedings and possible return to prison.

If the Parole Board denies discretionary release, reasons are given and a new consideration date is established which, by law, can be no more than two years hence. For inmates denied discretionary release by the Parole Board, statutory conditional release to community supervision may occur as the result of credit for good behavior ("good time") as early as service of two-thirds of the maximum sentence.

Victim Impact Initiatives

In May 1991, the Board of Parole initiated a pilot project which provided victims of certain violent crimes or their representatives the opportunity to meet with a member of the Board of Parole in a setting that promotes communication in a non-threatening atmosphere. In 1993, as a follow-up to Governor Cuomo's "State of the State" message, the Board of Parole restructured the 1991 pilot project and created a New York State Board of Parole Victim Input and Participation (V.I.P.) Program. This program ensures that those who wish to do so have an opportunity for input and participation if they or their loved ones become victims of violent crime.

Victim Participation

The Board of Parole welcomes the input and participation of the crime victim or, where the crime victim may be deceased or is mentally or physically incapacitated, their representative. A crime victim's representative has been defined as the crime victim's closest surviving relative or the legal representative of the victim. Typically, the input and participation may be in the form of a written victim impact statement or a personal statement during a meeting with a member of the Board of Parole.

Regardless of the format, all victim impact statements will be available for review by the panel of the Parole Board considering the inmate's case and will be one of the factors used to determine the disposition of the case. Anyone who has provided a victim impact statement will be advised of the case decision made by the Parole Board.

At some point during the prosecution of the defendant, the district attorney's office will provide the victim or their representative with a multi-purpose pamphlet concerning the New York State Board of Parole V.I.P. Program. If the victim or representative is interested in either submitting a written victim impact statement or participating in a personal meeting with a member of the Board of Parole, they should follow the instructions contained in the "V.I.P." pamphlet or, in the event a pamphlet is unavailable, simply state their request for input and/or participation in a letter mailed to:

N.Y.S. Board of Parole

Victim Impact Unit – V.I.P.

97 Central Avenue

Albany, New York 12206

Notes

Chapter 4
Letters to the board and press

Kathleen Connelly Takats 7/21/07

SID#

DIN#

Dear Respected Commissioners,

I come to you again, for the fourth time, and can only hope to come to you twenty more times because I will then know that John Duffy/ John Marino will be almost 90 years old and still behind bars (where he belongs). I recently purchased another life insurance policy and it runs to age 115, at least I have been given the chance to attempt to live that long whereas my brother, Jimmy Connelly, murdered at age 15 in 1979 by Duffy/Marino did not get the opportunity to really live at all.

I have written letters and made a video with my mother in the past to try to share with the parole board the sorrow and misery that still lingers in our lives from when Duffy/Marino brutally chased and butchered my brother, Jimmy's beautiful body and soul.

Jimmy was clean of all drugs and alcohol, as per the medical examiner's testimony at trial (exhibit 1) which is enclosed and states that no drugs, alcohol, or other mind-altering chemicals were found in him (please see page 384). My brother never drank or had done drugs in the past.

In addition, John Duffy's statement about never having an altercation with my family during the trial is completely false. He once blew kisses toward me and I yelled at him at the first bail hearing. I was devastated and shocked that I received contempt of court. When the DA learned of what happened from the court officers, the DA's office gave me the trial minutes (normally a $1500 charge) at no cost. These minutes were useful to show John Duffy's continuous lying under oath. They are currently in my possession (#2 receipt). John Duffy claims to have forgotten that incident and also forgets all of the people he spoke to minutes after murdering my brother; Testimony exhibit 3. Metal detectors had to be installed at the trial in 1982 when Duffy slapped me, ripped my coat, and punched me in the chest outside the courtroom. He cursed at my dad once again and I was so fed up that I slapped Duffy and told him to shut his mouth. John Duffy mocked and insulted me by saying "boo-hoo your brother is dead. You're next" and pretended to slash his neck. The court officers pulled him off of me and held my dad back. Judge McCarty stated in his 2005 letter that after seeing Duffy's poor behavior in court, his psychological pathology would not be cured in prison. Duffy and his family taunt us and the court officers despise them. The complete lack of remorse on the part of John Duffy is appalling and deserves a maximum life sentence.

Jimmy Connelly was a kindhearted kid and would never hurt another person. He was loved by many and the priest at his funeral called him a Prince of Peace. Jimmy was found with heavy suede gloves on with no blood on them or his wrists. He never had the chance to fight back or would have pulled the knife away from John Duffy/Marino. Duffy ambushed Jimmy Connelly. It did not faze John Duffy that he was only inches away from my brother's dying body, but continuously stabbed him in the back, chest, and neck. Duffy chose to use a knife as a murder weapon, the most personal and intimate weapon one could use, to slaughter my brother. (Review page 985). I also strongly believe that Duffy tried to sexually assault my brother and was fearful that Jimmy would contact authorities and slander Duffy's name. Inhumanly, Duffy killed my brother, Jimmy Connelly, in the worst way possible and lied to the Judge stating that a homosexual man pushed Jimmy's head into his lap which made Jimmy run away (exhibit 3). Please read his testimony enclosed (page 1037). My brother was unconscious from Duffy's blow to the head when the rest of the stabbing took place. Duffy then stole my brother's wallet to slow down the identification process when Jimmy's body was found. John Duffy was sickeningly able to ravage through my brother's torn, bloody clothing to find Jimmy's wallet without feeling an ounce of remorse.

After the murder, the first call Duffy made was to Fountain Auto Body where his family hid him for months.(More crimes, I am sure, were committed while he was in hiding- my next project to discover.) His stepfather, Ed Marino allowed him to hide out and use his name as a false identity for Duffy to go by. (Exhibit 4).

To this day, Duffy states that no one has ever asked him why he killed Jimmy Connelly or how he could commit such a crime, as stated at his past parole hearing. Is his mother brain dead? How do you not ask your son, while he has been in prison for almost 30 years, what went wrong!? This could, of course, be yet another lie on Duffy's part because he was surely asked in court and by the parole board why he murdered Jimmy Connelly.

Duffy's mother goes online to lookup my family on the "Parents of Murdered Children" website, which specifically states that you do not belong there unless you intend to help victims. At the last hearing she gave Duffy some private petition information; Maybe she should talk to her son about why he should remain in prison. Also, Duffy's sister, Colleen, died last July leaving behind five children while John's brother, Jimmy Duffy, had a jail sentence with John Duffy at Arthur Kill Prison. He lived a life filled with criminal offenses. Now, Duffy has no siblings alive. This is not shocking evidence because of Margaret Duffy, their mother, who led a life filled with mobsters and married, Ed Marino, a criminal activist as documented in trial transcripts and letters from Detectives on case. I submit Mr. Corr's testimony (page 1032) when Duffy told Corr's that he would "like to kill the kid" only an hour after he murdered Jimmy. Mr. Scrubbi's cousins stated that Ed Marino wanted to put them away and were terribly afraid of him (Duffy's step father). Please review page 1005 of testimony. In addition, Duffy told Garrapolo that he "stuck it to the kid" and "stabbed Jimmy a few times"! Garrapolo then went on the run with Ed Marino's help, because he feared for his life. In addition, while on bail Duffy was arrested twice for punching and robbing a woman, but used Marino for help and mysteriously fell through the legal system cracks. Duffy always used Marino's name when it suited him. Yet another fraudulent offense.

John Duffy's predominant connections to the mob are evident in the "Duffy-Cross" Defense case exhibited on page 787-790. Evidence proves that two phone calls were made to the Fountain Auto Sales in New York City the morning after the murder whereby his uncle and boss, John Coniglia, received the calls. Coniglia is known for his work in organized crime and has been in prison for extended periods of time. John Duffy called his boss Coniglia, a mobster affiliate, immediately after he murdered Jimmy Connelly and then hid out at the Auto Body Shop for several days. Duffy stated, Coniglia is "a good friend to the family, my sister's very good friend." Duffy has major organized crime connections and has been raised to confide and befriend criminals. How can Duffy therefore be eligible to be a law abiding citizen when he has been surrounded by men in organized crime for his entire life? He can NEVER and will NEVER be an abiding, productive member of society.

How do I suffer from the loss of my brother? Let me attempt to explain my grief. My dad suffered his first massive heart attack after seeing Jimmy's body in the morgue which put him in the hospital for 28 days. This caused him the inability to ever work again. My Dad's heart was working at only 17% and there were no medical options for him in 1979. My family and I were devastated with the death of my brother and the quick, eminent hospitalization of my father.

I wake up from nightmares of John Duffy being released from prison; Scared for my siblings, scared for my mother, scared for my children. I can never get even with that bastard and I cannot bring Jimmy back into our lives. Duffy is a man that haunts the Connelly family forever and I will always have a piece of my heart missing from the destruction he has caused me. I pray for Duffy's death. I have tried counseling, acupuncture, at night I rip my hair out in frustration, and I get hives that actually distort my lips and eyes. It's called anger, "great anger and rage." John Duffy tried to cut my brother's head off. Why? So my brother could never tell, that's why. Again, I believe that Duffy tried to sexually assault Jimmy Connelly and when he was unsuccessful, Duffy became enraged and viciously killed my brother. A simple fender-bender on a 300 dollar car while Duffy worked at an Auto-Body shop does not render murder. Duffy's possible attempt of sexual assault would. Please examine the story that he created while under oath about the "homosexual men attack."

Do you know what John Duffy did to us? He broke us; Each of us. He ripped our souls and punched our hearts. My brother, Terry, was eight years old, his brother gone forever. Patti and Barbara were young girls, worried that Duffy would come after them at night. I prayed for my Dad to live, I knew he was dying because of the devastation John Duffy caused my family. I went to court everyday with my dad and grieved. Barbara did not want to go in to the funeral home because she was beside herself in tears. My mother's son, her baby boy, murdered; her husband dying from the emotional destruction Duffy caused. We are afraid to let our children out of our sight. I just recently let my daughter go to British Columbia on a plane to ski at Whistler Mountain with the Okemo Mountain Alpine Racing Association. My husband and daughter had to beg me and I finally agreed, but thought of the dangers instead of the opportunities at hand. What we went through as children, as a family, is unbelievable. I hate to be called beautiful because Duffy used that as his nickname for me. I am trying to garden, sew, draw and not be so angry and remind myself everyday that justice is being served with Duffy behind bars.

The financial strain that Duffy has burdened my family with is worth acknowledging. There was barely enough money for us to survive because it was not an accidental death, it was a murder. My dad's insurance policy did not pay for any of the expenses because it was not an accident. Sometimes we went without food, without Christmas and birthday gifts. I was responsible for answering the calls from bill collectors. All of us children worked to support and help our parents. My dad died at age 43 of a heart attack that was initiated at the morgue where he had to witness his son's slashed body. We all broke our backs and got into college and paid on our own. Duffy goes to art classes in prison, eats daily, exercises, and works. Keep him there. Can't you see all the family criminal history? He is destined for a life of crime. In prison he is more productive, and my family can go on living knowing that he is behind bars.

After 26 years the DA, Judge McCarty, Nassau Court District Attorney's Office, and attending officers, states that John Duffy continues to lie to the parole board. He blames everyone but himself. I blame him fully and his crime infested family. Maybe he will start to realize, after 28 years, what he really did. According to the autopsy reports, John Duffy stood on top of my brother's body and made a "beautiful pattern over my brother's heart" as to cut it out. Duffy was only a few feet from my brother's pleading face and still continued to stab him over and over again. Duffy did not shoot my brother from a distance, but chased Jimmy down, stabbed him in the back and neck, turned him over and repeatedly stabbed him in the chest and then took two slices at my brother's throat. For supporting evidence refer to page 1048 & 1054. The workings of only a pure psychopath who NEVER deserves parole.

Before you consider John Duffy's well put together parole package think about my safety and the safety of others. Duffy has already threatened me by saying that he will "stab me and cut my throat." Can you imagine John Duffy blowing kisses and making obscene gestures at me while at a murder trial for my brother!? The psychological ramifications of this murder are uncanny. I demand to be heard and will fight against John Duffy until the day I die. In order to keep my family and I safe, the law must punish John Duffy to the fullest degree because of the absolute detriment he has caused us. Please, I beg you, protect us from this monster and make Jimmy Connelly's life a cause for celebration instead of a victim of vicious murder.

"**Psychopathy** is currently defined in psychiatry as a condition characterized by lack of empathy or conscience, and poor impulse control or manipulative behaviors. What is missing, in other words, are the very qualities that allow a human being to live in social harmony."

Thank you,

Kathleen Connelly Takats

Jimmy Connelly's Sister

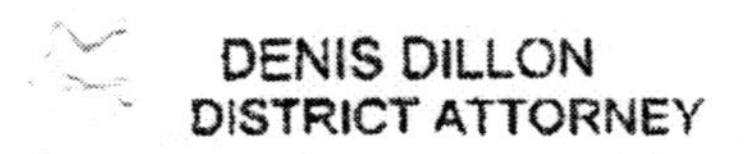

DENIS DILLON
DISTRICT ATTORNEY

OFFICE OF THE DISTRICT ATTORNEY
NASSAU COUNTY

262 OLD COUNTRY ROAD
MINEOLA, NEW YORK 11501 - 4251
TELEPHONE (516) 571-3800

November 2, 2005

FPO Joseph Sly, II
NYS Division of Parole
Arthur Kill Correctional facility
2911 Arthur Kill Road
Staten Island, NY 10309-1197

Re: People v JOHN DUFFY
(a/k/a) John Marino
NYSID #
DIN #

Dear FPO Sly:

We have previously written a letter opposing John Duffy's release on parole. Ordinarily, we do not submit additional letters on the same defendant. After reading defendant's testimony at his last Parole hearing, however, we wanted to inform you that his testimony is replete with lies and demonstrates that, although 26 years have passed since he killed James Connelly, defendant is still not taking responsibility for his actions. You should consider this in the future in determining the accuracy and sincerity of what defendant tells you.

In his testimony before the Board on August 29, 2005, defendant claimed to have used drugs the day he committed the murder (although he is quoted in the presentence report as using drugs the day before the murder) and had no recollection of the stabbing. At no time prior to his conviction did defendant state this and it is disproved by the facts. The wounds to the victim were not the type that are inflicted by a person who is under the influence of drugs, ie, random, scattered and disorganized. As you can see from the enclosed autopsy photographs (exhibit 1), the wounds are narrowly clustered and targeted to specific areas of the victim's body where they were likely to be most lethal, ie, neck, chest and back. Moreover, the lack of any wounds which would have been consistent with the victim trying to defend himself, eg, arms, hands and fingers, indicates the suddenness of the attack and is inconsistent with defendant's present claim that he took the knife away from the victim before stabbing him.

Also in his recent hearing testimony, defendant denied the highly inculpatory fact that he stabbed the victim while the latter was running away, claiming that the blood leading to the body was from his own injuries. This is specifically disproved by scientific evidence that the blood trail was of the victim's blood type (type O) and not defendant's (type A), that the victim was stabbed in the back several times and by defendant's trial testimony in which he described his only injury as being "no big cut, it was just like a little scratch on the top of the finger." Defendant also testified in the recent hearing, in response to a question from Commissioner Ferguson, that he did not lie to the police the night of the murder, claiming to have already fled the area by the time of that interview. However, PO James Freeman of the Suffolk County Police Department testified at the trial that he personally interviewed the defendant the night of the murder and that he specifically denied that he was involved in the car crash that led to the murder.

Most important, however, are defendant's present lies about why he admittedly perjured himself at his trial. He blames this on his attorney who is now deceased. An examination of defendant's trial testimony (summary attached as Exhibit 2) shows an elaborate, detailed and creative attempt by him in court to avoid conviction for this crime after already eluding capture by the police for 18 months. This is not the sort of defense that could be suggested by an attorney.* His present effort to shift responsibility for his own perjury to his dead attorney demonstrates that he is still attempting to avoid responsibility for his conduct and is not a reliable candidate for parole. He lied at the trial to avoid prison and again lied at his recent parole appearance to get out of prison.

Certainly, as we previously wrote, the murder itself justifies defendant's incarceration for the maximum term. This new information based upon defendant's recent testimony only reinforces our prior position that defendant still cannot be trusted to live among law abiding citizens. Accordingly, we recommend that his future parole requests be denied.

Very truly yours,

DENIS DILLON
District Attorney

Patrick J. McCormack
Chief Assistant District Attorney

PJM:sm

*In 1984 defendant filed an affidavit (exhibit 3) in which he criticized this same attorney for being so sick during the trial that he rendered incompetent counsel by allowing him to testify. Where was the present claim that the testimony was orchestrated by the attorney? When that strategy did not work, he told a different lie to the parole board.

August 28, 2003

To: Senior Parole Officer Ralph Rahm, Director Parole Board
From: Ret. Det. John Dabrowski, Homicide Squad, NCPD
Subject: John Duffy A.K.A. John Marino
ID NYSID:
DIN:

On January23, 1979, I was assigned to investigate the death of James Connelly. At approximately 4:15 am, James Connelly, a fifteen year old boy, was found dead by a garbage truck driver in the roadway adjacent to the Long Island Expressway, Plainview, NY.

James Connelly was stabbed multiple times and his throat was slashed. There was a blood trail of approximately 750 feet. This evidence establishes that James Connelly's murderer continued to viciously stab him as he attempted to flee.

As the investigation was being conducted, Mr. and Mrs. Connelly coincidentally came upon the scene looking for their son. The Connellys were told by Joseph Garappola, an associate of John Duffy/John Marino, that James Connelly had stolen Mr. Garappola's automobile and that he may be in the area of Plainview, NY.

The investigation led to Mr. Garappola's home in Center Moriches, NY and Mr. Joseph Garappola stated that Duffy/Marino told him that James Connelly had an accident with his automobile. Duffy/Marino told Mr. Garappola that he and James Connelly had a fight over the matter and he left Connelly in Plainview, NY and that Connelly was hurt and bleeding. Prior to the incident, they were drinking beer and playing pool in a pool hall on South Oyster Bay Road in Plainview, NY.

Mr. Garappola stated that Duffy/Marino told him to lie to the Connelly family when they came looking for their son. Duffy/Marino told Mr. Garappola to tell them that James stole his car while you were at work in Plainview, NY.

Mr.Garappola stated that Duffy/Marino made a phone call from his home and left for New York City on the Long Island Railroad.

The phone call was traced to an auto body shop which was operated by J[illegible] Coniglia, a reputed crime boss in the John Gotti organized crime family. Mr. Coniglia is presently serving life in a federal prison.

It was also learned that John Duffy assumed the name John Marino, after a reputed crime figure in the aforementioned organized crime family based in Howard Beach, NY. At that time, John Duffy's mother was living with John Marino nearby.

Duffy/Marino disappeared for the next 18 months. Our investigation revealed that he was being assisted in hiding by members of organized crime. The investigation to locate Duffy/Marino led to Florida, Howard Beach, NY, the auto body shop, Cross Bay Diner, and other locations notoriously frequented by members of organized crime. The constant pressure on the associates of Duffy/Marino forced him to surrender, upon the advice of his counsel.

During the trial, the star witness Joseph Garappola disappeared. Mr. Garappola's testimony would have been devastating to Duffy/Marino. Mr. Joseph Garappola appeared back in New York after the trial stating that he was in Florida. He said that his vacation was paid for by someone who he refused to name. It was also intimated that Mr. Joseph Garappola, Sr. was allegedly a connected mob figure to John Marino, Sr.

During the trial, Duffy/Marino testified that homosexuals picked him and James Connelly up and that they killed Connelly - a complete lie, knowing that Joseph Garappola was a missing witness. This statement was a complete lie, given under oath at the time of trial. If Mr. Garappola was available to testify, his testimony would have contradicted this farce. Despite the perjury of Duffy/Marino, the abundance of evidence against him proved to a jury of his peers that he was guilty beyond a reasonable doubt.

Duffy/Marino was convicted after trial and it was discovered that while he was out on bail, he committed two crimes in New York City. The Nassau County P.D. was never notified of these arrests. If the police department or courts had been notified, Duffy/Marino's bail would have been revoked.

I believe that the release of Duffy/Marino is not appropriate at this time for the following reasons:

1. The murder of James Connelly, age 15, was a vicious crime, in which his throat was slashed and he was stabbed numerous times, even after he had tried to flee his attacker;
2. The flight of Duffy/Marino for 18 months while hiding out in Florida and supplied with money from organized crime figures;
3. The lies at his trial;
4. Mr. Marino's disrespect to the judicial system was evidenced by hiding a potential witness in Florida so he could not testify against him;
5. His two arrests while out on bail seem to show he suffers from recidivism and demonstrates his inability to live within the bounds of law and society;
6. It is likely that Duffy/Marino will return to his previous lawless behavior and former associates, making it impossible for him to be a productive member of society;
7. Duffy/Marino will attempt to blame his vicious and brutal behavior on the use of drugs. He will claim that he is sorry and would never do this again. These statements to this board will be those undoubtedly scripted by his counsel and do not reflect his true vicious and unapologetic nature. Please do not be fooled by such theatrics and instead rely upon reason and common sense when deciding this matter.

Ret. Det. John Dabrowski, Homicide Squad

NCPD, New York

SUPREME COURT OF THE STATE OF NEW YORK
JUSTICE CHAMBERS
MINEOLA, NEW YORK 11501

October 16, 2005

Commissioner Robert Dennison
New York State Division of Parole
State of New York – Executive Department
97 Central Avenue
Albany, New York 12206

Re: Inmate John Duffy a/k/a John Marino
DIN___ NYSID___

Dear Commissioner Dennison:

In the early 1980's I was placed in charge of the investigation into the death of James Connelly. I was present at the murder scene and later observed the autopsy of this 15 year old teenager. He was stabbed over 20 times in the chest and had numerous stab wounds to his scalp and back. It was one of the most horrendous murders I have experienced in my 14 years as a homicide prosecutor. The attack was an exhibition of uncontrollable rage by the assailant and disclosed significant psychological pathology. I personally prosecuted John Duffy a/k/a John Marino. I observed his demeanor in the courtroom and can testify that at the time of the trial he still represented a significant risk to society. I do not believe his psychological infirmities would be subject to cure in a prison environment. I strongly believe that if released John Duffy would again exhibit his lack of self control which led to the death of James Connelly. Society would be at risk if he were released from incarceration. Please feel free to request any more information which may be of aid in your parole evaluation. I remain

Sincerely,

Edward W. McCarty III

My mother, Barbara Connelly's first letter to the Parole Board

Today is July 25, 2001, two days before the first parole hearing for Duffy. I am trying to put the important points down so as not to rattle off. It is so hard to try to write about this. I can only say that there are no words or scenarios to explain the trauma of the last 22 years.

John Duffy is a liar, thief, conniver, coward, and a spoiled, violent person with no regard for rules. He is a cold blooded murderer.

A liar, because with his lies to the police he was able to deflect suspicion, if any, away from him and onto Jimmy by saying he stole Joe's car. That gave him the opportunity to run and elude police and detectives for 18 months. He lied while out on bail for Jimmy's murder and gave a different name when apprehended for another crime, robbery and attempted murder! His bail was never revoked. It should have been; he tried to kill again! He is still a liar in jail. Don't be fooled by him. We are not.

A thief, because he stole Jimmy's wallet so as not to be linked to the crime of murder. He stole Jimmy's life, he robbed us all of peace forever. He stole our lives as we knew them when he stabbed Jimmy to death. He tried to steal another person's life. He still is a thief in jail. Don't be fooled by him. We are not!

A conniver, because at his bail hearing his attorney told the judge he had been working for family, and to please give him no bail. He is a good, hardworking person. Number one, he was on the run, so the whole family was lying. They too are liars and connivers like him. John Duffy told Detective Dabrowski "you were once so close to me in my relative's house, I could have breathed on you." He blew kisses to my daughter Kathleen at that bail hearing. She yelled out and the Judge held her in contempt, fined her $100 and let the conniver out on bail! He refused to come to his sentencing – it was postponed 3 times. He stayed in his cell! He still connives in jail. Don't be fooled by him. We are not.

A coward, because John Duffy chased a child. He left a child in the gutter, bleeding to death, running away while thinking about how he could get away with his act. In jail he is quick to get put in lock up or his cell. He doesn't want anyone to get him like he got Jimmy and that lady! Don't let him fool you. He does not fool us.

A spoiled, violent person when he didn't get his way. The story is that he wanted Jimmy to take blame for damage to a car and when he didn't get his way, he struck out at him, or maybe he will tell you the real story. When the lady didn't give up her money or whatever else he wanted, he assaulted her. When a witness in the case, Joe Garappola was going to appear in court, he and/or his family threatened his life and he fled. When he doesn't get his way, he acts out. He has done this in jail. Don't let him fool you. He hasn't fooled us.

A cold-blooded murderer, he chased and slaughtered our first born son. He chased him 354 feet, so they say, stabbing him repeatedly, stopping only when Jimmy fell and then cut his throat. For several years my sleep was interrupted by scenes I imagined. I had to make a pact with God - if I continued to say my prayers until I fell asleep, would he please keep that scene out of my head? I still pray until I fall asleep and God has kept his part. Duffy has been found with items to make weapons in jail. Don't be fooled by him. We are not.

What can I say to you to let you know how important it is to our family that he is denied this parole?

Let me tell you how my husband was affected. A 35-year-young dad had a major heart attack! He was unable to work again. The thief stole his right to provide and protect! He couldn't go to work; his boss fired him because he was unable to complete a day's work in the first week after he returned to work. He was in the hospital for one month! My husband was taking 13 pills a day and was on Valium for his anxiety. He never even took an aspirin in all of our 17 years of marriage. Disability took 6 months to finally get, then it went on only for about 6 months. We had to apply for Social Service. We couldn't pay our mortgage! We had no health insurance! And everyone got sick that first year and was hospitalized, except Patti.

One day we tried to buy a used car from a dealer. We had the car home and they towed it out of the driveway the next day. They said a credit report came up that we owed a funeral bill. We explained the situation. Jimmy was murdered and the insurance didn't pay but we paid it off with Social Security benefits. They said if someone didn't pay their child's funeral bill, how could anyone ever trust them to pay for a car? We never knew that the funeral home had taken a lien against us. We had to go to them, tell them what happened, and then get a letter from them that they were paid. We had to file it in Riverhead!

Over these years, we were so desperately financially deficit that I got a job housecleaning. I couldn't get a real job as my children were still young and Jim wasn't well enough to take care of them for a long time. Although I got Kathy out to school in the morning, Jim got Terry out to school and Patti and Barbara got themselves out. It was a chore to get just Kathy out. I would fall onto the couch everyday after she left as if I had done hours of hard work. I really don't know how we survived! We just did.

One day I contacted a doctor to speak to. I knew we were in trouble but I didn't know what to do. I had to make a decision whether to put the only $5 we had into gas and go to the doctor or buy chopped meat for dinner. We had nothing in our usually overfilled pantry. I opted for the doctor; I knew if I didn't I would never be able to make dinner again. He asked me how he could help us. I asked if he ever had a family who had a child die the way Jimmy did. He said, "No, I never have." I said, "Do you know our lives have changed forever?!" He just looked at me. I had only bullion cubes to give the kids for supper! Can you keep this thought in your head while you contemplate Duffy's parole? Duffy created hell for us! Hell on earth!

There is so much to tell that there is not enough time – you know that and I know that. How can I explain to you how my Jimmy's murder impacted upon me and my family? It killed my husband! It stole every breath of our lives. It took the light and left only dark in our eyes. We love and laugh with a reservoir of unimaginable pain.

I lost my home when my husband died at age 43. I was 45. I tried to manage to keep it, I had a full-time job, but it wasn't enough. John Duffy is responsible no matter what way you look at it, cut it, or push it around. This is a direct result of his actions. Other than whatever restitutions he had to pay in jail, he doesn't pay medical bills, utility bills, or shelter bills. He will never have to pay restitution for Jimmy's funeral bill. He cannot repay his debt to our family by being released. He can only do that by staying in jail for the entire length of his sentence. He took Jimmy's life with death, he took our lives as we knew them, and he gave us a life sentence to never be paroled. He deserves to pay his debt to our family. We are society! His debt to us can never be over. Ever.

I know he has manipulated the system, he is good at it. He is in a drug program in Arthur Kill, a facility that is ten times better than where he was. He is geographically closer to his family. I want him back in a Maxi Max.

How will this Parole Board explain to another victim's family that he was released because of his "good behavior?" I doubt he has had good behavior in jail; you had better keep him there because he didn't have good behavior when he was on the street. He and his family threatened my husband and daughter. They would make fun of me in the hall of the court as we went through the trial. I was never allowed in. Sometimes I would be crying. They would look at me and rub their eyes and say, "Boo hoo hoo." Duffy grabbed my daughter Kathleen at one of those times and ripped her coat. I scratched his face with my ring and told him that he would NEVER hurt another one of my kids. He just laughed at me. The guards separated us. I was not allowed in and his whole family in their leather coats came everyday. They are part of some organized crime family. I know it and so does the Nassau County District Attorneys Office. I have never contacted him in prison, I never wished him evil. I only said, "Let happen to him what is supposed to happen to him for what he did."

Twenty years cannot be enough for what he did!

My first major hurdle: How do you set a dinner table for 6 when you have set it for 7 for so long? We lit a candle and put it in his place; I was crying and shaking with sobs. A candle, where a boy should be eating and laughing. Why did my children have to see their mother and father so distraught? Twenty years is not enough for that!

Our family has used these last 22 years positively; we have helped so many others. That is not a reason to keep him in. It is a fact.

We used our 20 years productively once he was convicted and sentenced. You and I cannot say he did the same.

Our family was able to go on with our lives while he was off the street. If you put him back out, it will set us back. I never knew that you didn't go to prison for life when you murdered someone. I was a Catechism teacher; I taught religion for 6 years. I never knew that life wasn't really life when you are a murderer.

Our family needs to have John Duffy behind bars so that we may continue to grow our families and do good things for others. All that will be impeded if he is released. He is not a good person. Remorse is not a word in his dictionary, and it is too late if it is.

I have left so much out, so many years of traumatic stress. Each member of our family suffers from Posttraumatic Stress Disorder. They have been manifested in so many different ways: physical stress, emotional distress, anxiety, denial and avoidance, intrusion, repetitive nightmares, impaired memory, loss of concentration, blaming oneself, reclusive behavior.

I didn't tell you how Jimmy loved Batman or how he had a photographic memory. I haven't told you how he wanted to make computers talk! Or how he worried about his sisters and brother and how he watched out for them. How he was good to his neighbors. I didn't get to tell you he was born early, walked early, talked early, and as you know, died early. I haven't told you how it feels being here without my husband. He fought so hard for Jimmy and all of our kids.

I'm not sure if I told you that I miss him so much, but I do know he is dead and not coming back. I remember that the toy dog he received as a gift from my sister Linda the day he was born is still here and Jimmy is not.

Letter to Parole Board re: Duffy, John 7/22/03
ID #
DIN
Dear Members of the Parole Board:

Terrorism, according to Webster's, is the systematic use of terror. To terrorize is to fill with terror or anxiety.

I come before you today to implore you not to release inmate John Duffy on parole. Duffy is an inherently evil man who mutilated and killed my kind, gregarious brother, James Connelly.

When I say John Duffy is evil, I do not use the word loosely. Just as those terrorists who murdered innocent people and attempted to kill America's spirit on 9/11 are evil, so is John Duffy. But Duffy did not kill my 15-year-old brother for money, religion, or revenge. He did it because human life has no meaning to him. He stabbed my beautiful brother more than 20 times and slit his throat twice. Since that horrific day, Duffy has continued to terrorize my family.

Duffy's brutal murder of my brother also led to my father's death. He suffered a heart attack after identifying my brother's body at the morgue and never worked again. Within six years he died; he was only 43. John Duffy is the sole reason that my mother had to mourn the loss of both her son and husband.

After the murder, Duffy was on the run from police for 18 months. His family has the means for him to disappear at any point in time. While he was on bail and awaiting trial, Duffy assaulted a woman. This is not a man who will be redeemed no matter how much he attempts to look good to the parole board. Duffy has no regard for human life, laws, or authority.

John Duffy is the reason that my family grew up with no emotional or financial security. He stripped us of that and never showed remorse. He laughed in our faces during the trial. He threatened and terrorized all of us. He is the reason each of my siblings, who ranged in age from 8 to 16 at the time of Jimmy's murder struggle with depression and anxiety to this day.

John Duffy's evil was not a fleeting thing. He physically assaulted me outside the courtroom with corrections officers right there. I was encouraged not to press charges because we feared the trial would end in mistrial. I am on record as having suffered at his hand and I will fear for my safety and the safety of my family if he is released. Duffy deserves to spend his life in prison where his erratic and dangerous behavior can be controlled. It is unfair to unleash such evil on innocent people.

I need to show you the ultimate example of the difference between good and evil. Evil is John Duffy. A cold blooded murdered who grew up with money and privilege and who chose to butcher a young boy for the sheer thrill of it.

Good, is my mother Barbara Connelly; an amazing woman who survived the brutal murder of her son, the loss of her husband, and infinite financial and emotional horror. Through it all, my mother chose to be good. She started a support group for parents of murdered children. She became a licensed grief counselor. She donates her time to make life more livable for those who aren't sure that they can make it through another day.

Since 9/11, my mother has donated her time to work with survivors of the terrorist attack. She has taken no money, though she could have been paid. She chooses to do this out of the goodness of her heart; a heart that has been broken by the evil bestowed on our family by John Duffy.

My family lived with the shadows of John Duffy's evil since the day he murdered my brother. The only peace that we have is in knowing that he is locked up. He assaulted and threatened me and I simply cannot handle any more terror. I should not have to. I am quite literally putting my life in your hands. I beg you not to release this evil man. He will terrorize again.

Sincerely,

Kathleen Connelly-Takats

Letter re: geographic restraints for John Duffy 7/24/03

ID#
DIN#

Dear Members of the Parole Board-

My name is Kathleen Takats. My wonderful, sweet, gregarious, 15-year-old brother, Jimmy Connelly, was brutally murdered by John Duffy. Duffy stabbed him more than 20 times and slit his throat twice. During the trial, Duffy continued to terrorize me and my family.

John Duffy never showed any remorse. He physically assaulted me outside the courtroom in front of corrections officers. He also threatened me and my family throughout the trial. I am on record as a victim of John Duffy's.

If there is any chance of Duffy being released from jail, I respectfully request the most stringent geographic restraints possible be placed on him to bar him from living anywhere near me or my family. I live on Long Island and my mother and siblings also live in the area. This evil man has terrorized us all and we suffer from anxiety and depression because of him.

I can't even consider that John Duffy may someday be free. But if that dreaded day ever comes, I pray that his parole includes geographic restraints. I don't know how my family could live through having this man anywhere near us.

Thank you for your consideration to this serious request.

Sincerely yours,

Kathleen Connelly-Takats

August 5, 2003

Dear Council Office,

My brother, Jimmy, was the victim of a terrible crime and his murderer is up for parole again. Commissioner Block has requested that we get the minutes from the last parole hearing. At the last hearing he admitted to killing my brother. Yet, he lied about who the knife belonged to. He claimed that it was my brother's knife. This proves that he is still a liar and a threat to society. He still has not taken complete responsibility for his actions. Commissioner Block thought that it was important for the parole officers to know what John Duffy did when he was on bail. On January 24, 1981, one year to the day that he killed my brother, he tried to do it again. John Duffy attacked a 40-year-old woman. He was arrested but used the alias of John Marino. The charges were later dropped because this woman had thought that he would be put away for life for the murder of my brother, and she couldn't bear to go through the pain and agony herself. Through the Freedom of Information Act, we are trying to get all of this information so we can present it to the parole board. His information is as follows:

Re: John Duffy
NYSID #
DIN #

Sincerely,

Kathleen Takats

Letter to Parole Board re: Duffy, John 8/5/01

ID #

DIN #

Dear members of the Parole Board:

The photo you see on my victim impact statement is of my sweet, kind, gregarious brother, Jimmy Connelly. Jimmy was brutally murdered on January 22, 1979 by an inherently evil man, John Duffy. Jimmy was 15 years old when John Duffy chased him down like a dog and literally, butchered him with a knife. Duffy stabbed Jimmy more than 20 times and slit his throat twice. For this crime, John Duffy received "20 years to life."

On behalf of Jimmy's family, friends, and the community at large, I am writing this letter to compel the parole board **not to release John Duffy** on parole.

Duffy's crime was so heinous it calls for a life sentence. Today, I believe John Duffy would be sentenced to die by lethal injection and we wouldn't have to fear that he would be free.

Words cannot convey the incredible amount of pain and suffering this man has caused. John Duffy cannot be handed the opportunity to inflict this fear and misery on any other individual or family.

John Duffy has never shown remorse. At the trial, he assaulted me and threatened my life in front of corrections officers who had to pull him off of me. (The DA sent you a letter asking you keep John Duffy in jail.) We could not press charges because the DA feared a mistrial.

John Duffy murdered my brother. Duffy also bears responsibility for my father's death. My dad suffered a major heart attack after identifying my brother's mutilated remains and died a few years later.

John Duffy is the reason my siblings and I, who ranged in age from 8 to 16 at the time of the murder, experienced indescribable pain while listening to my mother sob uncontrollably every night.

John Duffy forced us to grow up without our brother and our father, without emotional or financial security. He has made us feel pain and stress everyday. When John Duffy murdered Jimmy, my mother was 35 years old and my father was 37. After my father's massive heart attack, he was never able to work again. He died at age 43.

My brother, Jimmy, was a wonderful boy. He was, as people always said, "a really good kid."

My family was always involved with the church and Jimmy served as an altar boy. Jimmy was never involved with drugs or crime of any kind. On the day he was murdered he was going to help a friend with a painting job.

After the murder, my family was plunged into emotional and financial ruin. As children, we worked after school to help bring in enough money for meals and gas. My mother cleaned houses.

Jimmy was my best friend; I miss him more than you can ever understand. Once, when Jimmy and I were little, I missed a parade I was supposed to march in. I was sad so my brother actually bought me a sympathy card to make me feel better. This is one small example of his kind and gentle spirit.

My siblings and I were all stripped of any feeling of personal safety. We knew at a young age that even parents couldn't protect you. My family continues to live with this dark cloud of evil shadowing our lives. Each of us struggles with depression and anxiety. The horrifying images of my brother being brutally attacked and dying alone in terror and agony haunt us all.

The only semblance of peace we have is in the knowledge that John Duffy remains in prison where he cannot harm others or us. Please don't take away our only bit of peace.

John Duffy's prison record is further proof of his contempt for authority, rules, and regulations. There are 165 pages of incident reports in his file. These include inmate misbehavior reports and unusual incident reports which detail accounts of fighting, confirmed drug and alcohol use, contraband razors, mirrors and broken Plexiglas (weapons), failure to follow direct orders, creating a disturbance/demonstration, failure to carry ID, failure to show up for work assignments, remaining in the officers' post area after being told no inmates can be there, and the list goes on.

John Duffy is a man who is incapable of remorse. He believes the rules of society and of the jail do not apply to him. As it states in one of the 165 pages of reports on Duffy, he was told he was in violation of a direct order to come out of his cell. His response was, "I don't give a fuck about direct orders."

John Duffy has no hard luck story of living on the streets. He grew up with money and privilege. He, alone, is responsible for his indifference to human life and that indifference makes him a danger to anyone who comes into contact with him. John Duffy has not "earned" release from prison. He continues to get what he believes he is entitled to through fear, intimidation, and violence. I don't believe he instills feelings of trust or reverence in many people. His own mother and sister refused to attend his trial. No one knows better than you, the high recidivism rate for felons, especially those who have no remorse. John Duffy savagely murdered an innocent boy IN COLD BLOOD. John Duffy laughed, taunted, and abused my family throughout his trial.

After the murder, Duffy fled to Florida where he remained for 18 months before he turned himself in. His family has the money and connections for him to be a flight risk at any point. John Duffy assaulted a woman while he was on bail. The DA informed us that while the woman was terrified to testify, she only dropped her case because she believed Duffy would receive a life sentence for murdering my brother. My brother's body was so badly mutilated by John Duffy that the funeral directors have written you a letter. The DA has also written a letter. I know you have received letters from family, friends, clergy, teachers, and elected officials. We all pray you will not set Duffy free.

This crime was so heinous that members of the church were compelled to implore you not to release Duffy from jail. Priests and nuns are the biggest believers in redemption. John Duffy has not fooled them. Please don't let him fool you. John Duffy gave our family a life sentence of suffering and misery. Do not allow this man the freedom to commit another heinous act. I beg you. I implore you. I plead with you. Do not let John Duffy go free. (I have enclosed 3 copies of our videotape and 4 additional letters.)

Sincerely yours,
Kathleen Connelly-Takats

Connelly Killer Up For Parole

For Immediate Release 7/13/05
Media contact: Sheryl Jenks

Justice Edward McCarty III said when John Duffy brutally mutilated and murdered 15-year-old Jimmy Connelly on a Plainview street in 1979, it was the most vicious attack he investigated in his 14 years as an Assistant District Attorney for Nassau County.

On Friday, July 15 , Connelly's family will appear before the Parole Boards' th Victim Impact Unit to implore the board to keep Duffy behind bars. Duffy, who the police department said has ties to "a reputed crime boss," is being considered for parole after serving 24 years of a 20 years to life sentence. Duffy was denied parole in 2001 and 2003.

According to Justice McCarty, "I observed the remains of James Connelly. He had been stabbed approximately 22 times in the chest and in excess of 10 times in the back. His scalp had been lacerated from the crown of the skull to the base of the skull. It was undoubtedly the most vicious attack I had observed in over 500 homicide investigations."

Duffy has shown no remorse for his heinous crime. He was on the run in Florida for 18 months after the murder before law enforcement closed in on him and during the trial he threatened Connelly's family and assaulted Connelly's sister.

The Connelly family, friends, police, members of the clergy, school district personnel, the District Attorney's office and elected officials have all written letters to the New York State Parole Board to contest Duffy's parole.

Connelly's sister, Kathleen Takats, will present damning evidence to the parole board regarding Duffy's continued lying and likeliness to commit other violent crimes if he is paroled.

"I have proof that Duffy lied outright to the board at his last parole hearing. He said he was never involved in any other crimes. My investigation proved that while on bail after murdering my brother, Duffy assaulted a 40-year-old woman. Three months later he was arrested again for violent behavior and resisting arrest," said Takats.

Retired Homicide Detective John Dabrowski talked about these crimes in a four page letter he wrote to the parole board outlining the many reasons he joined the family's fight to keep Duffy behind bars.

"After trial it was discovered that while on bail, Duffy committed two crimes in New York. If the courts had been notified, John Duffy/John Marino's bail would have been revoked." Dabrowski wrote.

"His two arrests while out on bail show he suffers from recidivism and demonstrate his inability to live within the bounds of law and society," Dabrowski wrote.

The Connelly family suffered incredible hardship after the murder. Connelly's father, 35 at the time of his son's murder, suffered a massive heart attack after identifying his son's mutilated body and died a few years later. The family was plunged into emotional and financial adversity.

Duffy's prison record includes 250 pages outlining drug and alcohol use, weapons and contraband, fighting and failing to follow direct orders.

"John Duffy is a cold-blooded murderer. He showed pure indifference to human life. He physically attacked my daughter, Kathy, and threatened our lives at the trial. John Duffy is the reason my husband is dead. Duffy never showed one drop of decency or remorse. He and his family taunted us during the trial. John Duffy is a menace to society. He must remain in prison," said Barbara Connelly of her son's murder.

"Jimmy was a wonderful, handsome boy who was always happy to help people. Twenty years after he was murdered I still couldn't throw away his clothing. His jeans, his pajamas, his navy blue Catholic school blazer, it was too much to bear. My daughter had the clothing turned into an amazing quilt and pillow. It means so much to me," Connelly said.

The family brought that quilt as well as family photos to their Victim Impact Hearings prior to Duffy's last two Parole Board Hearings.

Barbara Connelly has spent her life helping other people who have experienced the horror of having a family member murdered. She was awarded the "Certificate of Special Congressional Recognition" after being chosen "Woman of the Year" 2000 for starting the first New York branch of "Parents of Murdered Children" as well as "Children Have Feelings, Too" support groups.

Connelly was designated the nation's 837 "Point of Light" by former President George Bush, was also chosen as "Newsday Volunteer" in 1992 and volunteered her time after the September 11 attack, working as a grief counselor for those who suffered losses.

Teddy's Time

Photo Courtesy Museum of Modern Art

Theodore Roosevelt at Grant's Tomb, 1910

100 Years Ago, McKinley Assassination Thrust Roosevelt Into the Presidency / Part 2

Jordan Encore?

AP Photo, 1998

Court Return Looks Likely

Sports

Newsday

THE LONG ISLAND NEWSPAPER

www.newsday.com TUESDAY, SEPT. 11, 2001 • SUFFOLK 50¢

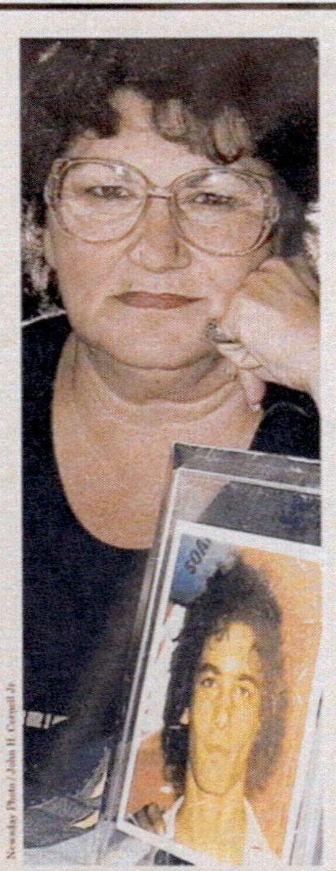

Newsday Photo / John H. Cornell Jr

Barbara Connelly of Shirley with photo of her son Jimmy, murdered 22 years ago

Nightmare Relived

Mom Battles Parole Bid By Her Son's Killer

Page A3

Israel's New Fear

THE Enemy

AP Photo

Muhammad Saker Salah Habashi, an Arab citizen of Israel

Within

Mistrust Deepens Inside Jewish State After Suicide Bomb Attack By an Israeli Arab

Page A5

Battling Parole Bid

Woman wants killer of her son to remain imprisoned

Newsday Photo / John H. Cornell Jr.

Newsday File Photo

John Duffy, above, after surrendering to authorities on July 9, 1980, in the slaying of Jimmy Connelly. At left, Jimmy's mom Barbara sits with a quilt made from her son's clothes.

Years ago, Barbara Connelly made a pact with God, which went something like this. She would say her prayers before she fell asleep, 50 or 100 "Our Fathers," and He would save her from her nightmare, the scene of her son running in the dark, being stabbed by another man.

Considering all she has endured in the 22 years since she lost her son, this was a small request. And she has found some peace over the years.

But for the past several months, Connelly, of Shirley, has been battling to keep the man of her nightmares from re-entering her world. John Duffy, the man sentenced to 20 years to life for stabbing Connelly's 15-year-old son more than 20 times, will make his case before the parole board this week.

As Connelly sees it, there's a clear relation between her family's sufferings — from the days spent in bed screaming her throat into hoarseness to her husband's death — and Duffy.

The 60-year-old Connelly, who founded the first metropolitan-area chapter of Parents of Murdered Children, insists she is not morose, not one to wallow in pity. But nothing can make up for the disintegration of her world, she said.

"It's all a direct result, a direct result," said Connelly. "I can't tell you how much he took from us. ... The 20 years he's [Duffy] been in prison it's given us the opportunity to live. I believe if they let him out, that will stop."

Connelly and her four remaining children are not alone in their quest to keep Duffy locked up in the medium-security Arthur Kill Correctional Facility.

Family priests, nuns, friends of the family, the Nassau County district attorney and even the funeral directors who tried to piece together Jimmy Connelly's battered body have inundated the board with letters.

Duffy could not be reached for comment.

The statistics don't favor Duffy's chances of freedom. From 1988 to 2000, the percentage of inmates convicted of first- and second-degree murder and attempted first-degree murder who were granted release hovered between 5 and 6 percent, said Thomas Grant, spokesman for the New York State Division of Parole. Duffy also has wracked up a string of disciplinary infractions over the past decade, ranging from drug use, harassment and refusing orders.

Yet, Barbara Connelly said she knows that Duffy's release during her lifetime is very possible. And if she has been successful at persuading the parole board to keep Duffy in prison this time by appearing before it, she said she will be ready to wage battle every two years at his hearings.

The crime itself was vicious. Among the 22 stab wounds on Jimmy Connelly's body, 10 were clustered in the chest area and two pierced his heart. His neck and head bore gashes. His skull was fractured and his throat slashed. Detectives traced blood back some 100 feet. Jimmy Connelly was running as he was attacked, they concluded.

"I saw a young man bleeding from his neck and head, blood flowing," said John Dabrowski, a retired Nassau County police detective turned private investigator who hasn't forgotten much about the case.

Connelly remembers her son's innocent request, which took him to Plainview on Jan. 22, 1979. Jimmy Connelly asked if he could help his friend Joey Garrapola paint his mother-in-law's apartment. Instead, Garrapola drove Connelly and another friend, Duffy, to his new job at a Plainview factory and loaned the two his car until he got off work.

Duffy and Jimmy passed the time at a bar and played pool, Dabrowski recalled. They later slammed the car into a utility pole and argued over who was responsible for the damage. That's when Duffy murdered Connelly, detectives say.

"I can't tell you what made this kid do it," Dabrowski said. "This was savage."

Duffy went into hiding for 18 months. Dabrowski and other detectives kept the pressure on Duffy's family members and friends. They flew to Florida in search of the then-19-year-old man. Until he turned himself in, Connelly and her family said, they lived in fear.

See PAROLE on A28

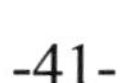

Mom Fights to Keep Son's Killer ... Prison

PAROLE from A3

Duffy would later claim during the trial that he and Connelly smashed Garrapola's car and hitched a ride with two homosexual men. They made advances and stabbed Connelly and he ran, he told the jurors. They didn't believe him.

The crime and the trial revealed the Connelly family's desperation and grieving. But what the public usually does not see and what other families of murder victims need to realize, Barbara Connelly said, are the long, private years of mourning.

She remembered the moments of isolation among the family members during those first terrible years, the falling apart of a family and the dire economic straits that nearly pushed the Connellys to the wall.

"We lived despite it all," Barbara Connelly said. "Everything we could have suffered, we suffered. No one knows how we took all of it. It's like you have no heart, but you breathe."

Jimmy Connelly was a sweet and caring kid, his sister Kathleen Takats recalled. He shunned disco for rock and roll, and loved the Doobie Brothers, his baby-blue corduroys and "Saturday Night Live." He dreamed of making computers talk, his mom said.

"He was just a boy," said Takats, 39, of Babylon. "He never made love to anybody. Who knew what he would become? He was just a boy."

Identifying their son's body triggered her husband's first heart attack, Barbara Connelly believes. James Connelly Sr. suffered another heart attack the day after Jimmy Connelly's funeral. A week later, he was hospitalized after suffering a third major heart attack. Upon his release three weeks later, the man who kept his pain to himself had lost his job as the manager of an electronics firm, with only a six-week severance package and a large family to feed, clothe and send to college.

The Connelly family nearly crumpled thinking about the mortgage, already several months late, and the funeral bill the insurance company would not pay because Jimmy Connelly's death was not an act of God, an accident or the result of an illness.

Nearly the entire family ended up at the hospital that year. The youngest, who was 8, had an appendectomy. Their 13-year-old daughter broke out in what doctors said were stress-related hives. Stress sent Takats to the emergency room and Barbara Connelly had screamed and cried her epiglottis almost completely shut.

Disability gave her husband $90 a week for six months. Barbara Connelly worked cleaning houses at first. Takats waited tables. And Barbara Connelly's parents helped out when they could.

Her husband died eight years later, at age 43.

Barbara Connelly said her family has moved on. All of her son's clothes have been sewn into a quilt. The black satin bat from the disco-shirt he hated, a patch from his favorite white, dungaree overalls, and his navy blazer from his Catholic-school uniform.

It gives her comfort reliving her life before her son's death. She can smooth the fabric as she used to after pulling her son's clothes from the dryer. She can pick lint from his navy blazer as she used to before he would shoot out the door to school.

This is the life she wants to revisit, she said. She wants no more interruptions.

NEWSDAY, TUESDAY, SEPTEMBER 11, 2001

To: Whom It May Concern

July 15th, 2005

Hello my name is Jessica Takats I am twelve years old, I am writing this letter in remembrance of my Uncle Jimmy Connelly who was murdered by a horrific man named John Duffy. I have been writing parole letters since I was in first grade and I was reflecting back on them all as I was writing this letter. My Mother, Grandmother, Aunts and Uncle had a really hard time after the murder of my Uncle Jimmy. It could be hard for anyone, but still my grandma made wonderful changes, the laws she changed after this tragic crime were un-countable, she organized the group " Children have Feelings Too", and takes a great part in "Parents of Murdered Children!!" Its almost as if she was a super-grandma you may call it! The entire Connelly family plus relatives and friends come together every two-years and almost as if relive this horrible tragedy of losing my uncle in a brutal murder But I know that every two- years my family keeps working in trying to keep John Duffy in jail! I really don't know how they all do it. I was looking through all documents and in a remembrance letter my mom's class-mates made for her in their high school my mom stated " Jimmy did you ever know you were my hero? " My uncles life ended so quickly he never got to know simple things like he was my moms hero, or that he would have nieces and nephews that truly love him, If my uncle never got to experience simple things as Christmas with all of the family then John Duffy shouldn't either because it was not my uncles fault he was killed that dreaded day it was John Duffy's , if he made the choice to kill my uncle with no reason, then he shouldn't have the chance to ever step out of jail again. See because if you have ever known anyone who had someone in their family murdered and still have to work every two-years to keep their killer in jail you would know how hard it is on the entire family. My family is truly amazing is the only word to describe them all! If you don't keep John Duffy in jail you are making a huge mistake, he has brought so much terror to our family and to many other people! As you are making your final decisions about this parole hearing I ask you to think if your brother, grandson, uncle, or nephew went out one day and never came back, and try to imagine what the Connelly's went through. I thank you for your time and please make the right decision.

In Loving Memory
of
Jimmy

Thank you,
Jessica Takats_ Who misses her Uncle

Notes

Chapter 5
Letters of support

NYS Division of Parole
Victim Impact Unit

Hearing September 2001

Re: John Duffy
NYSID
DIN #

Victim: James Francis Connelly-D.O.M. January 22/23, 1979

I am writing to NYS Division of Parole so you **deny** any opportunity of release for John Duffy. My name is Joseph D. Glasson. I am the surviving cousin of Jimmy. Jimmy was like a big brother and idol to me. I was about 13 years old when this happened and I still feel the pain today. The pain I feel is for the loss of a brother. The anguish I feel is for my Aunt Barbara who has relived his death every day; never a day goes by that she doesn't feel sorrow for the wrongful brutal murder of her son.

Aunt Barbara asked me to write to you about how Jimmy's death affected my life. How does anyone deal with a brutal murder? Death alone is very hard for loved ones but a wrongful brutal murder of a 15-year-old boy should not even be up for discussion. How can you possibly let this animal back on the streets? So 20 years has gone by and some may think he has paid his debt to society, but what about his debt to our family? The hardship it put on my Uncle Jim's heart, which eventually killed him, the pain my aunt goes through every day, the pain and the fear my cousins go through knowing this animal threatened them when he gets out. Please understand the pain is still very real for my family and it will never go away. I am trying to keep this as direct as possible but let it be known that many of us would like to deal with Duffy ourselves, but as a good and fair human being, I hope the laws of our land will do the right thing and keep him behind bars for the rest of his life.

To: NYS Board of Parole June 17, 2001

Victim Impact Unit
97 Central Avenue
Albany, NY 12206

From: Kostanti and Barbara Kruk Re: John Duffy
I.D. #:

To Whom It May Concern:

It is our understanding that John Duffy is eligible for parole in the fatal death of James Connelly. This heinous crime occurred on January 22, 1979. Our involvement in this case stems from our personal, as well as professional, relationship with the Connelly family.

Having known the family from our church and community affiliations, we were called upon at the time of Jimmy's death to take charge of his remains and funeral arrangements. We owned the funeral home that took care of the remains.

As funeral directors we have seen much tragedy in the course of our professional career, however, the body of young James Connelly was so mutilated it was difficult for us to prepare the remains for open visitation. After many long, tedious hours of restorative reconstruction we were able to afford the family the opportunity to have an open casket. The task was emotionally and physically daunting. Jimmy had been an extraordinarily handsome boy, his slim but muscular physique had been nearly destroyed.

The entire community was shocked and gripped with fear. John Duffy was at lodge for over a year. No one knew where or when he would surface or who, would become his next victim.

The pain at the loss of his son, and namesake, was the cause for the heart attack suffered by Jim, senior. He was never the same after his son died. His mother, Barbara, has fought tirelessly to help counsel the parents and families of other murdered children. Her efforts, and those of the rest of her family, are well known in our community. It has been our honor and privilege to work side by side with this brave survivor.

Please accept this letter as our petition for the denial of release for John Duffy. Young Jimmy Connelly has not been paroled from his death sentence, why should John Duffy.

On January 22, 1979, John Duffy murdered many people. Twenty years is not long enough to forget or erase in our minds the sight of Jimmy's tortured body. Our only hope is that John Duffy never forgets.

Thank you for your consideration of this plea not to release John Duffy.

Very truly yours,

Kostanti Anthony Kruk
Barbara Guarino Kruk

NYS Division of Parole
Victim Impact Unit

Re: John Duffy
NYSID
DIN#

Parole Board,

The night before we found out my nephew Jimmy was murdered, my sister called to ask me if Jimmy was with me. He hadn't come home when he was supposed to and they hadn't heard from him since about six or seven that evening. She said someone told her Jimmy stole a car and they figured he would come to me in Boston. Jimmy didn't drive, never had an interest as far as I knew and I knew him pretty well.

He was my Godson, we were close. I loved him, spoiled him, and played with him (horsy back rides when I was eight months pregnant with my own son). He came in the summers for a week or two. We did so many things together.

When he was growing up and got hurt or someone called him a name or someone was mean to him, I would become so angry at that person or persons that they would think twice about doing it again.

When they went to school (Jimmy and his sisters) in the Bronx, I walked with them and my sister everyday. The Bronx was starting to become a bad place at that time and kids were being beaten up for their coats, sneakers, and lunch money. They went to Catholic school and we lived in the better part of the Bronx, but it was still bad. I wore a shoulder holster and carried a gun to protect them if I had to.

When they called and told us that Jim-Jim had been murdered, stabbed by someone, I did not believe it. All around me my brothers and sisters were screaming and crying. My mother almost passed out and I had to calm them down. I had to tell my father when he came home from work that his grandson was dead.

Later on that night we found out to what extent he had been stabbed and I thought, "My God, this isn't true!" Why hasn't Barbara called me? If I could just talk to her this would go away. I had only talked to my brother-in-law that day. I wanted to talk to my sister. I had to know – SHE had to tell me.

I was Auntie Linda; I protected my nieces and nephews, my brothers and sisters, my child. I was the one that got furious over any injustices done to any of them.

I didn't cry, scream, or pass out. I didn't want to walk into that funeral parlor. I could only remember when my sister was looking to buy a house in that area and found what she wanted; as we passed that funeral parlor she said to me, "I wonder who will be the first to go there." I said, "Oh, shut up. You're so morbid."

I did not want to walk in there! But my brother-in-law made me; he and my niece, Kathleen, walked me in. I didn't cry, I didn't scream, and I didn't pass out. I said to Jimmy when I leaned over the casket to kiss him, "Auntie is so sorry Jim-Jim, I'm so sorry." I WAS so sorry! I was so sorry I wasn't there to protect him. I was so sorry I hadn't been able to prevent this from happening. I was so sorry I had moved back to Boston because if I had stayed with my sister, my nephew would still be alive.

When the trial came, my sister asked me not to come to it. She did not want anything to jeopardize Duffy's right to a fair trial. She wanted to be fair. I wanted him dead!

He stole the light out of my niece's eyes, he stole her personality, he ripped my sister's heart out, and he took from her the ability to remember the simplest things. Her words were gone; they would come and go. He took my brother-in-law's life because when we buried my nephew, my brother-in-law had a heart attack and never, ever recovered from it. He died at the age of 43. He took away a little brother, a big brother, the first born grandson, a wonderful cousin, he took away a favored nephew, and he took away a Godchild.

He took away my child's right to grow up not worrying that his mother was going to go off half crocked because someone looked at him the wrong way. He took away my child's right to go fishing or to the movies with his friends at 12 years old without his mother being one step behind him. He took away our God-given right to live in peace.

Peace is gone and never has come back. We live in fear of every stranger around our children. He took away our dreams and replaced them with nightmares. This is 22 years later and I do not allow my grandchildren to ride their bikes farther than the stop sign. I don't allow them to go around the side of my house because I can't see them there. I don't allow them to be out of my sight. While all the other children are playing around the corner, they have to stay in the backyard.
Twenty-two years later and I haven't learned to trust anyone or anything. THAT'S BEEN MY LIFE! The anger and rage I have in my life and cannot get rid of, John Duffy gave to me.
When you confront John Duffy at his hearing, please look at him with your ears and not your eyes and you will hear the screams my nephew must have screamed while John Duffy was doing his thing. Listen to these letters you receive with your eyes and you will see the pain, anxiety, sorrow, and heartache that he caused so many people.
I ask you as an aunt, mother, sister, and Godmother not to release John Duffy. My nephew received the death penalty for doing nothing wrong at all. John Duffy has served only 20 years. Please listen to this letter and don't hear my rage and anger. Instead, please see my heartache and sorrow. My name is Linda Policastro and I am the aunt and Godmother of James Francis Connelly.

Thank you,
Linda Policastro

STATE OF NEW YORK
DEPARTMENT OF CORRECTIONAL SERVICES
THE HARRIMAN STATE CAMPUS
1220 WASHINGTON AVENUE
ALBANY, NY 12226-2050

October 2, 2001

Ms. Patricia Connelly

Re: Inmate John Duffy
DIN #

Dear Ms. Connelly:

Governor Pataki has asked me to respond to the recent letters you and your mother sent to him respectively as the sister and mother of James Francis Connelly, who was murdered by inmate John Duffy in 1979. You described in graphic detail the circumstances surrounding the brutal murder of James Connelly and the behavior of John Duffy during the pendency of the criminal trial, which culminated in his conviction for murder in the second degree and a sentence of twenty years to life. You express vehement opposition to the potential release on parole of inmate Duffy and you also question how he was allowed to be transferred from a maximum security prison to his present facility, Arthur Kill, which is a medium security facility, and where he has been allowed to participate in a drug treatment program.

First, let me express my sincere condolences over the loss of your brother. I have worked within the field of corrections for nearly thirty years and during this period, I have received countless letters from crime victims and their family members. Unequivocally, the most compelling and moving letters that I receive are from the family members of homicide victims, especially from the parents of homicide victims. I know all too well that no matter what else happens, nothing will ever bring back the deceased, and that regardless of how much time elapses, the pain endured by the family will never be lessened.

While I am aware that you have already had the opportunity to express your opinions to the Division of Parole with regard to inmate Duffy's upcoming consideration for parole release, nevertheless, to ensure that there is no possibility for an oversight, I have instructed my Counsel, Anthony Annucci, to contact his counterpart at that agency, Terry Tracy, and to forward to him copies of your letters. Mr. Tracy, in turn, will see to it that the facility parole officer has these letters as part of the official record for when inmate Duffy appears before the Board of Parole, which because of the events at the World Trade Center, has been postponed until next month.

OFFICE OF THE DISTRICT ATTORNEY
NASSAU COUNTY
262 OLD COUNTRY ROAD
MINEOLA, NEW YORK 11501
TELEPHONE (516) 571-3800

February 16, 1999

FPO Joseph Sly
Arthur Kill Correctional Facility
2911 Arthur Kill Road
Staten Island, NY 10309-1197

Re: People v. JOHN DUFFY
Indictment No.
NYSID #
DIN #
Date Convicted 01/29/82

Dear Officer Sly:

We are in receipt of your letter pertaining to this inmate. Please be advised that we are respectfully opposed to his release on parole supervision.

On January 23, 1979, the defendant, JOHN DUFFY, brutally attacked and murdered 15-year-old James Connelly. On the night of the homicide, it is believed the defendant had an argument with the victim. The defendant stabbed the victim twenty times: six wounds in the back consistent with the victim being stabbed as he fled; three slash wounds on the neck severing both the jugular vein and carotid artery; ten wounds to the chest, eight in the lungs and two in the heart and a slash in the back of his head. The victim also sustained a fractured skull. The defendant fled the scene and it was not until eighteen months after the crime that the defendant finally surrendered.

The defendant brutally cut short the life of a 15-year-old. Twenty years have passed since the defendant committed this crime and the victim's family remains devastated by it. There is nothing in the defendant's background nor in the circumstances of this case that warrant favorable consideration by the Board of Parole. We would request, therefore, that his application for release to parole supervision be denied, and that he be compelled to serve the maximum term permitted by law.

Very truly yours,

DENIS DILLON
District Attorney

Harvey B. Levinson
Chief Assistant District Attorney

OFFICE OF THE COUNTY EXECUTIVE
One West Street
Mineola, New York 11501

June 12, 2001

New York State Division of Parole
97 Central Avenue
Albany, New York 12206
Att: Martin Cirincione, Executive Director

Dear Mr. Cirincione,

It has come to my attention that an individual currently housed at the Arthur Kill Prison in Staten Island is being considered for release on parole. This prisoner's identification numbers are NYS ___and Din#___. This individual was convicted of the murder of James, son of Barbara Connelly of _______.

I have been asked by Mrs. Connelly to recommend that parole for this person be denied. I ask that you give all due consideration to the suffering Mrs. Connelly and James' family have endured.

THOMAS S. GULOTTA
County Executive

DeFilippo Family

June 17, 2001

NYS Board of Parole
Victim Impact Unit
97 Central Avenue
Albany, NY 12206

Dear Board:

We are writing to express our deepest concern for John Duffy's possible upcoming parole (NYSID ___ DIN#___). It is our belief that John Duffy should serve his full prison term for the violent crime that he committed. John Duffy is a killer and has proven that he can and will kill again. Jimmy Connelly lost his life in a most violent nature at a very young age and John Duffy should not have a free life of his own. Other family members have had their lives threatened by John Duffy as well. We have confidence that you will consider our concern when John Duffy comes up for parole.

Sincerely,

The DeFilippo Family

THE ASSEMBLY
STATE OF NEW YORK
ALBANY

June 22, 2001

Mr. Brian D. Travis, Chairperson
New York State Division of Parole
97 Central Avenue
Albany, NY 12206

Dear Mr. Travis,

I write with regard to John Duffy (A.K.A. John Marino, NYSID___ DIN#___) who is serving a twenty years to life sentence.

On January 22, 1979, fifteen year old James Connelly was brutally murdered by John Duffy. The nature of this crime was so horrific that James' father, then age 35, suffered a major heart attack the day following his son's funeral. Unable to work, Mr. Connelly died at age 43.

My understanding is that a parole hearing is scheduled for John Duffy in September. On behalf of Barbara Connelly (James' mother) and her family, I appeal to you, in the strongest possible way, to deny this dangerous and violent offender from being granted parole. In addition, I ask you to keep in mind that at the time of the trial, John Duffy threatened to kill other members of the Connelly family.

The Connelly family has suffered immense loss and should not be subjected to additional fears with the release of John Duffy.

Your serious consideration of these facts is most appreciated.

Sincerely,

Thomas P. DiNapoli
Member of Assembly

Notes

Chapter 6
Letters of recognition

COUNTY OF SUFFOLK
OFFICE OF DISTRICT ATTORNEY

THOMAS J. SPOTA
DISTRICT ATTORNEY

VICTIM ASSISTANCE PROGRAM

February 13, 2002

Fleet Bank

To Whom It May Concern:

I have been advised that you have nominated Kathleen Connelly-Takats for an award honoring her contributions and service to the community.

In my position as Victim Services Coordinator for the Suffolk County District Attorney's Offi have had much experience with the organization, Parent of Murdered Children over the past 13 years. From 1985-1997, Ms. Connelly-Takats' mother, Barbara Connelly, chaired that organizati Parents of Murdered Children provides support and information to families dealing with the murc of a loved one. While Mrs. Connelly chaired the group, her daughter provided support to the organization in many important ways, such as financial contributions, technical support, and most importantly emotional support to victims. Ms. Connelly-Takats started the first siblings group of Parents of Murdered Children filling a very important need that had not been specifically address prior to her doing this. The siblings group became a very strong branch of Parents of Murdered Children with her guidance and direction.

I'm sure that Ms. Connelly-Takats brings the same enthusiasm and commitment to the busines community as well. I applaud your recognizing such a deserving person for this award.

Sincerely,

Anna M. Audioun
Victims Services Coordinator

CRIMINAL COURTS BUILDING • 200 CENTER DRIVE • RIVERHEAD, NY 11901-3388 • (631) 852-2551

Certificate of Special Congressional Recognition

Presented to:

Barbara Connelly

"Woman of the Year" 2000

September 14, 2000
Date

Member of Congress

STATE OF NEW YORK

GEORGE E. PATAKI
GOVERNOR

September 14, 2000

Dear Friends:

It is a pleasure to offer greetings to all those gathered for the Women of the Year Awards Banquet sponsored by Women of Substance.

Women of Substance is an organization whose commitment to increasing awareness for such issues as domestic violence, substance abuse, breast cancer, emotional stress and other health related concerns of women is truly commendable. I join in congratulating this year's honorees Barbara Connelly, Cheryl Leisa Williams, Diane Dunne, Rosalie G. Rose, Vestine Bryant and Sandy Seltzer. As role models in their respective professions and areas of expertise, your award recipients are deserving of the accolades bestowed upon them from Women of Substance and the community at large.

Best wishes to all for an enjoyable and successful event.

Very truly yours,

George E. Pataki

I

COUNTY OF SUFFOLK

Robert J. Gaffney
COUNTY EXECUTIVE

Dear Friends,

Please allow me to offer my sincere congratulations to Women of Substance on the occasion of your annual "Woman of the Year Awards Banquet," Congratulations, also, to your most deserving award winners this year.

The recipient of your "Woman of the Year" 2000 Award. Ms Barbara Connelly, is truly inspiring Ms. Connelly, having suffered through the brutal and senseless murder of her teen aged son, helped form the Long island Chapter of "Parents of Murdered Children," Throughout the years she has worked tirelessly to obtain funding and assorted grants for families who have been forced to endure the tragedy of losing a child at the hands of another,

Her caring and loving manner coupled with her intense desire to help others, clearly demonstrates why she is a most worthy recipient of this covered honor. I convey u« her my thanks and those of the 1.4 million residents of our County.

Sincerely,

ROBERT J. GAFFNEY
Suffolk County Executive

Notes

Chapter 7
A time for change

A jail sentence of twenty years to life is not enough time for murder. I don't understand how a criminal can receive a mere 15 year sentence for a crime as heinous as murder. The fact that two years is considered the maximum amount of time for a criminal to be up for parole baffles me. Some are even offered parole in as little as six months- I cannot even imagine going through this process that often. We have to congregate together and demand for changes in our legal system on a federal and state level. You can begin lobbying for law changes by joining a self help group such as the National Organization for Victim Assistance at *www.trynova.org*, the National Center for Victims of Crime at *www.ncvc.org*, and the National Victims' Rights Constitutional Amendment Network at *www.nvcan.org*. My parents helped form one of the first groups in the tri-state area called Parents of Murdered Children, where they lobbied for change in legislation through Congress. In addition, by accessing the National Organization for Parents of Murdered Children at *www.pomc.org*, you can post parole block petitions to foster awareness of your case on a national level. You may also find other chapters of POMC in your area and connect with families of similar circumstances.

Congress must be aware of just how painful, exhausting, and excruciating parole hearings are for the victim's family. I was not fully at peace knowing that every few years I would have to repeat my attempt to keep my brother's killer in jail. My uneasiness has stayed with me, but I know that I must continue to fight his parole; otherwise he is likely to be released. By articulating and communicating the destruction that is rooted in our lives and expressing the sadness that still lingers from the past, the board will continue to acknowledge my plea. Your presence is necessary at the parole hearing so that the board can realize the full impact of the crime. Stay strong, utilize your close friends and family for support, and ask them to help you gather some of this information so you do not feel stressed. My family and I were blessed to have such wonderful people speak on our behalf at Duffy's parole hearing. They handled our case with such care and dignity which must have been overwhelming for them as well; God bless them. I hope you have similar outstanding individuals to help you with this arduous task.

I believe that knowledge is power and by spreading the important information that I have learned and experienced, you too can successfully triumph in your parole hearings. The circumstances that we face in our daily lives should not define who we are as people, but should empower us and make us achieve greatness. I hope that in the least, I have provided you with some assistance to the methods and process of acquiring data and information to support your case. Your loved one deserves it. Cherish the memories that you shared and remember to laugh, love, and live the best way you can - everyday.

"Although the world is full of suffering, it is also full of overcoming it." – Helen Keller

Our primary goal is to reach out to the survivors of a victim of violent crime.

CVOC/POMV's objective is to provide understanding, comfort and support in the face of tragedy, to assist survivors to reconnect with their families and their communities with the strength necessary to survive the murder of a loved one.

Since 1981 many of our members have met once a month in an effort to reach out and allow a survivor to express his/her feelings, and to experience being part of a unique community. We provide a network of those who know what survivors are living through.

We continually provide information on what to expect from the justice system ie: what to expect at trials and how in the future to circumvent parole release.

CVOC/POMV produces and circulates its own quarterly newsletter and holds an annual vigil/dinner during National Crime Victims Week (usually held in April).
We draw together in December to share in a non-denominational holiday meeting.

As survivors and advocates
we present at conferences, seminars, media events. We help to educate school personnel and employers. We share the hardship survivors of murdered victims go through each and every day. This provides the helping fields (public and/or private) the tools to enables survivors of murdered victims to reorganize and/or regroup in the face of a tragic event. To begin life anew.

We provide crisis intervention with certified volunteers.
We are available 24 hours a day for telephone contact

Outreach for the Secondary Victim

CVOC/POMV receives approximately 20 phone calls a day.
We serve 5% of our membership every 5 days.

We share in approximately 200 – 300 members at a Vigil/dinner each year.

POMV Provides service to 75% to 100% of our members every year by participating in:

a. training for new DA's in New York State, provide sensitivity training as they come in contact with our members and our future New York members
b. in the New York State Police Cadets trainings.
c. attending at least three to four murder trials each year in New York State.
d. monthly meetings serving approximately 20 –30 members on an average.

Whether it be at our homes, on our own phones, computers and faxes or at our regular jobs utilizing our work time to serve survivors.

Long Range Goals

Present an Annual New York State Conference

To inform, educate and offer support for all counties of New York

Strive to leave no survivor of a homicide victim behind.

www.linypomvoutreach @aol.com

We are an all Volunteer Tax Exempt (501c3) Not For Profit Organization.

If you wish to make a tax exempt donation

POMV/CVOC Outreach Inc

107 Venetian Promenade

Lindenhurst, NY 11757

Name...

Address...

State....... Zip.......

$........... Check#..............

In Memory Of

....

....

No cash please.

LONG ISLAND NEW YORK METRO AREA PARENTS AND OTHER SURVIVORS OF MURDERED VICTIMS OUTREACH INC.

(POMV)

Serving Families and Friends of Murdered Victims and Victims of Violent Crime

Executive Director

Barbara Connelly

631-395-3820 - Fax 631-399-6544

Chapter leader

Christine Baumgardt

631-957-8376

Notes

Chapter 8
Stress Management Tips

- A punching bag
- Relaxing music before bed and if necessary, while sleeping can help relieve tension
- A blue light, which is a night light that helps aid sleep
- Reflect upon your past memories that have positively influenced your life.
- Exercise, exercise, exercise; the more vigorous the better. It is a proven, all-natural, stress reducing activity
- Do outdoor activities such as skiing, biking, walking, running, or gardening to enjoy nature while clearing your mind at the same time
- Keep pictures and memorabilia of your loved ones around the house
- Preserve items (such as clothing, pictures, or books) that your loved ones cherished
- Pick up a new hobby or advance an old hobby that has always interested you
- Join a community outreach program on a topic that interests you (such as neighborhood watch, environmental restoration, or volunteer work)

You have to learn a new way to live after the loss of a loved one. Continue to be the best mother, father, brother, or sister that you can be and live each day with hope, faith, and love. Reducing your levels of stress will be the first step to revitalizing your own life. It is up to you to cherish your loved one's memory and keep their spirit alive. God bless my family as they strive to accomplish this everyday.

This photograph of the bi-centennial, and more importantly of the Twin Towers, was given to me as a gift from my brother, Terry. In 1976, my mother took us children to view the tall ships off the coast of the Hudson River. I have such fond memories of Jimmy enjoying the ships and had always admired the World Trade Center.

The enormity of the picture has caused many to express their grievances regarding the loss of friends and family from the 9/11 attacks and I will never forget when a retired policeman came over and shared his story from that tragic day. He explained how he carried many children to safety from the preschool and day care center located within the Twin Towers and how grateful he was to have saved as many lives as he could that day.

His story made me upset and yet angry at the idea that the attacks on our country were from soulless individuals who did not care about destroying the lives of innocent civilians and their families. I reflected upon the memories of those lost and truly believe that we all owe each other collectively to make this country a better place.

Notes

Acknowledgment

I would like to thank all of my friends and family who have supported me through this experience and offered their help during the parole hearings, particularly the Nassau County DA office, Honorable Justice Edward McCarty III, and the respected Detective Dabrowski. Special thanks to my husband Scott, daughter Jessica, and son James, for always being there for me during these difficult times.

Thank you to Sherry Jenks who assisted with creating media documents and writing letters for the first few hearings, and to June Jacobson for her photography.

Special thanks to co-author J. Hayes for spending countless hours writing and editing my letters and this book.